W9-CKT-497

THE ROCK CYCLE

by Martha London

The Child's World®
childsworld.com

Published by The Child's World®
1980 Lookout Drive • Mankato, MN 56003-1705
800-599-READ • www.childsworld.com

Photographs ©: Shutterstock Images, cover
(foreground), cover (background), 1 (foreground,)
1 (background), 11, 19, 20 (top), 20 (bottom right),
20 (bottom left); iStockphoto, 5, 20 (middle
right); David Parker Photography/Shutterstock
Images, 7; Ralf Lehmann/Shutterstock Images,
9; Doug Meek/Shutterstock Images, 12; Jodie
Johnson/iStockphoto, 15; Bjoern Wylexich/
Shutterstock Images, 16; Ekkaluck Sangkla/
Shutterstock Images, 20 (middle left)

ISBN 9781503828506
LCCN 2018945375

Printed in the United States of America
PA02396

About the Author

Martha London loves writing books for
young readers. Martha lives in Minnesota
and has one cat, Zee.

Table of Contents

CHAPTER ONE
What Is the Rock Cycle?

There are three basic types of rocks on Earth: **igneous**, **sedimentary**, and **metamorphic**. Each type of rock is different. They form at different places on Earth. Some are formed far below the ground. Others are formed above ground. The rock cycle shows how the different types of rocks can change into each other. The cycle takes millions of years. Even though the process is long, people can still see the rock cycle at work. Wind and rain play a part in the cycle. People walking in a field or cars driving on the road also play a part in the rock cycle.

Rocks are made up of many different minerals. Minerals are hard like rocks, but minerals are made from **elements**. Elements cannot be broken down into any other particles.

Rocks are everywhere. People can pick up rocks in yards or parks.

CHAPTER TWO
Igneous Rocks

Igneous rocks are often formed under Earth's surface. The Earth's core is very hot. It is hot enough to melt rock. This melted rock is called **magma**. When magma cools enough to become solid again, it becomes igneous rock.

Sometimes magma settles and cools below ground. This slow cooling creates an igneous rock called granite. The continents are made up of a lot of granite. Granite is very durable. This makes it ideal for making buildings and bridges. Mount Rushmore is a famous memorial. It is carved from a massive granite mountain in South Dakota.

Four former presidents are carved into the igneous rock at Mount Rushmore.

Magma can push up through the layers of Earth. It comes out in the form of lava when a volcano erupts! Lava cools very quickly when this happens. This fast-cooling lava, combined with gas bubbles, makes air pockets. The air makes some igneous rocks **porous**. The holes that form in rocks make the stone rough. One example of this type of stone are pumice rocks. Some people use pumice rocks to smooth rough skin on their feet.

Most volcanic eruptions happen in the ocean. The ocean floor is made of an igneous rock called basalt. Basalt is also found on volcanic islands such as Hawaii.

Igneous rocks can change when they are exposed to **weathering** and **erosion**. Weathering and erosion start the process of creating sedimentary rocks.

Lava in Hawaii has been known to reach 1,165 degrees Fahrenheit (629°C).

9

CHAPTER THREE
Sedimentary Rocks

Sedimentary rocks are made of tiny pieces called sediments. Some of these pieces are small grains of sand. Some are larger. Sediments come from different rocks, such as igneous rocks.

Tiny bits break off rocks all the time. This process is called weathering. It is caused by water and wind. Temperature or chemical changes can also break apart rocks. When these tiny rock pieces are moved, it is known as erosion. For example, rivers can pick up and move pieces of rocks.

Over long periods of time, sediments can settle into layers.

Weathering and erosion are only the first steps in making sedimentary rocks. When rock fragments settle at the bottom of a hill or on the floor of the ocean or lake, the next step in the process can begin. This process is called cementation. The bits of rock press together over time and become one rock. Sometimes animals that die get buried under the sediments. This is what makes fossils!

Weathering and erosion caused by the Colorado River helped form the Grand Canyon.

CHAPTER FOUR
Metamorphic Rocks

Metamorphic rocks form when igneous or sedimentary rocks become very hot and are pressed very hard. The word *metamorphic* means "to change form." The combination of heat and pressure changes the structure of the minerals in the rocks. This can happen at the bottom of the ocean floor or on **tectonic plates**. The transformation into metamorphic rocks takes place without the rocks ever melting. If they did, that would mean they would eventually become igneous rocks.

Tectonic plates are often made up of igneous rocks. When tectonic plates crash against each other, their weight creates a lot of pressure. The **friction** of the plates sliding over each other creates heat. Sometimes one of the plates rises.

Metamorphic rocks can be found in kitchens. Marble is often used as a countertop.

Are Diamonds Metamorphic Rocks?

Diamonds are made through extreme heat and pressure. That sounds a lot like a metamorphic rock! But diamonds are not rocks. They are minerals. Diamonds can be found in an igneous rock called kimberlite.

Sliding plates might make a mountain range. The heat and pressure that comes from creating a mountain will change the structure of the minerals in the plates. This change transforms an igneous rock into a metamorphic one. The type of metamorphic rock that is formed depends on the type of minerals in the igneous and sedimentary rocks.

There are many examples of igneous and sedimentary rocks becoming metamorphic rocks. Marble is a metamorphic rock. It began as limestone, which is a sedimentary rock. Many statues are carved from marble. Another type of metamorphic rock called gneiss began as the igneous rock granite.

Diamonds must be polished and cut before they are made into jewelry.

Metamorphic rocks can be very beautiful. They can be brightly colored. Sometimes people use them in jewelry. Lapis lazuli is one example. It is blue and can be polished so that it is shiny. People have been making jewelry out of lapis lazuli for more than 6,000 years.

It is difficult to separate each type of rock because they are all dependent on each other. The rock cycle explains how each rock can be transformed into a different one and back. Igneous rocks form when sedimentary and metamorphic rocks are melted down and then harden. Metamorphic rocks form when igneous and sedimentary rocks are pressed and heated so that the minerals change shape! Sedimentary rocks are formed from the weathering and erosion of metamorphic and igneous rocks. None of these rocks would exist without the others.

Lapis lazuli can be made into necklaces.

The Rock Cycle

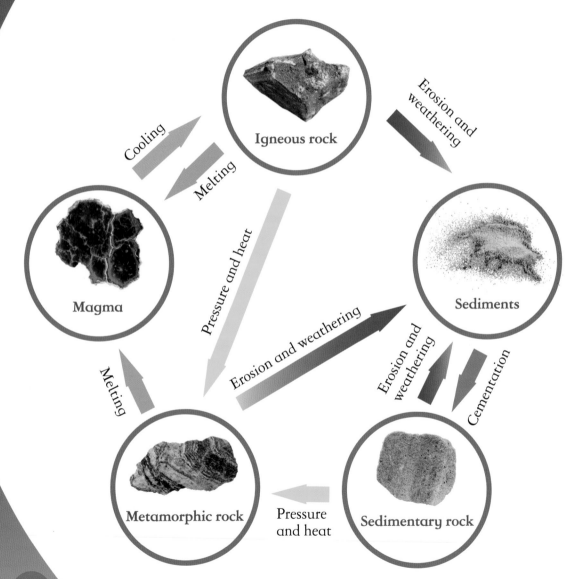

Cooling

Igneous rock

Erosion and weathering

Melting

Magma

Pressure and heat

Sediments

Erosion and weathering

Erosion and weathering

Cementation

Melting

Metamorphic rock

Pressure and heat

Sedimentary rock

Fast Facts

- There are three basic types of rocks: igneous, sedimentary, and metamorphic. These rocks can change into each other.

- Sedimentary rocks are created when sediments of metamorphic and igneous rocks go through the cementation process. Metamorphic rocks are made through the heating and squeezing of igneous and sedimentary rocks. When metamorphic and sedimentary rocks melt and eventually cool, igneous rocks are formed.

- Rocks are more than just a part of the landscape. People rely on rocks for the construction of buildings. Rocks can also be made into jewelry.

Glossary

elements (EL-uh-muhntz) Elements are substances that can't be broken down into smaller substances. Minerals are made up of elements.

erosion (i-ROW-shun) Erosion occurs when pieces of rocks are carried away after they have been loosened by weathering. Rivers can be part of the erosion process.

friction (FRIK-shun) Friction is when one object rubs against another and encounters resistance. Tectonic plates create friction when they crash together.

igneous (IG-nee-us) Igneous rocks form when melted rock cools. Most of the ocean floor is made from igneous rocks.

magma (MAG-muh) Magma is melted rock found in Earth's core. Magma can cool below ground and form granite.

metamorphic (met-uh-MOR-fik) Metamorphic rocks are created through heat and pressure. The metamorphic rock marble began as the sedimentary rock limestone.

porous (POR-us) Something that is porous has many small holes. Porous rocks are rough.

sedimentary (sed-uh-MEN-tur-ee) Sedimentary rocks are made from fragments of larger rocks. Sandstone is one type of sedimentary rock.

tectonic plates (tek-TAHN-ik PLAYTZ) Tectonic plates are massive areas in Earth's crust that move. Tectonic plates play a role in creating rocks.

weathering (WEH-ther-ing) Weathering is the process through which small pieces break off rocks. Weathering helps create sedimentary rocks.

To Learn More

IN THE LIBRARY

Lawrence, Ellen. *How Do Water and Wind Change Rock?: A Look at Sedimentary Rock*. New York, NY: Bearport Publishing, 2015.

Rajczak Nelson, Kristen. *What are Metamorphic Rocks?* New York, NY: Gareth Stevens Publishing, 2018.

York, M. J. *Igneous Rocks*. Mankato, MN: The Child's World, 2017.

ON THE WEB

Visit our Web site for links about the rock cycle:
childsworld.com/links

Note to Parents, Teachers, and Librarians: We routinely verify our Web links to make sure they are safe and active sites. So encourage your readers to check them out!

Index